My First Visit to Hospital

Rebecca Hunter

Photography by Chris Fairclough

Evans

Published in paperback by Evans Brothers Ltd in 2004
2A Portman Mansions
Chiltern Street
London WIU 6NR
England

First published in 2000

Hunter, Rebecca
My first visit to hospital, - (First Time)
1. Hospitals - Juvenile literature
1. Title
362.1,1

ISBN 0 237 52694 8

Acknowledgements
Planning and production by Discovery Books
Editor: Rebecca Hunter
Photographer: Chris Fairclough
Designer: Ian Winton
Consultant: Cheryl Hooper B.A. (Hons) is a Director of Action for Sick Children,
the leading children's healthcare charity in the UK. The charity specialises in establishing
good practice in children's health services, provides information and support to parents
and has been at the forefront of many changes to children's healthcare in the NHS today.

The publishers would like to thank Jonathan Drewek, Els and Karl Drewek, Jane Jackson,
Hazel McNinch and the staff of The Royal Surrey Hospital, Guildford
for their help in the preparation of this book.

My First Visit to Hospital

My name is Jonathan.
This book tells you about
my first visit to hospital.

Contents

I have to go to hospital.

I cannot hear very well. The doctor said I need grommets in my ears to help me hear better. I will have to go to hospital.

We get ready to go.

I am not allowed to eat anything before my operation. Mum helps me pack my bag. I'm hungry!

We arrive at the ward.

Dad takes me to the hospital. We meet the nurse who will look after me. She is called Hazel.

Hazel examines me.

First of all Hazel weighs me.

Then she measures my blood pressure and takes my temperature.

I have a bracelet with my name on it.

Hazel writes my name on a plastic bracelet.

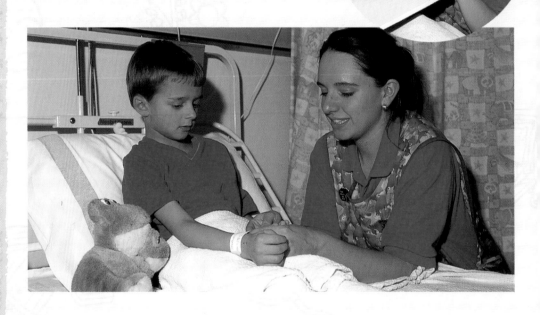

She puts it on my wrist so that everyone will know who I am.

We meet the doctor.

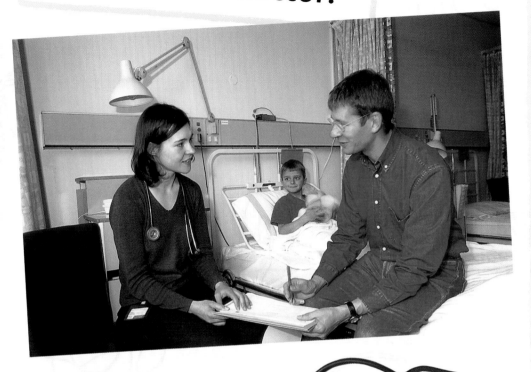

The doctor comes and tells Dad and me what is going to happen. Dad has to sign some forms.

I put on a theatre gown.

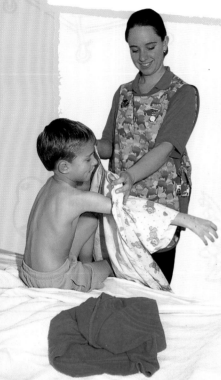

Hazel helps me put on a funny shirt called a theatre gown. I will wear it in the operating theatre.

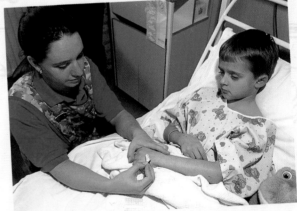

She puts some cream on my hand so the anaesthetic injection won't hurt.

My bed turns into a trolley.

Hazel turns my bed
into a trolley.
She and Dad
wheel me down
the corridor.

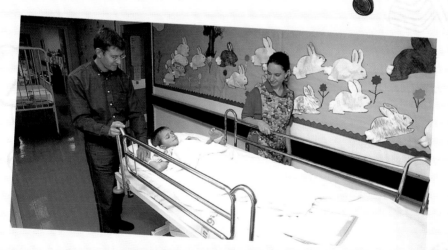

I like the children's
pictures on the walls.

I have an injection.

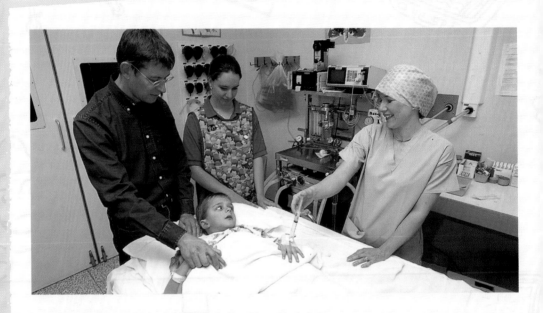

The anaesthetist gives me an injection which will make me go to sleep. The needle didn't hurt.

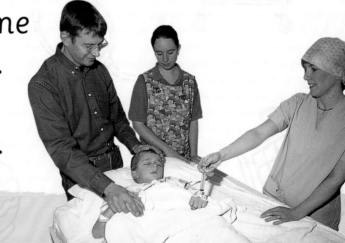

My operation is over.

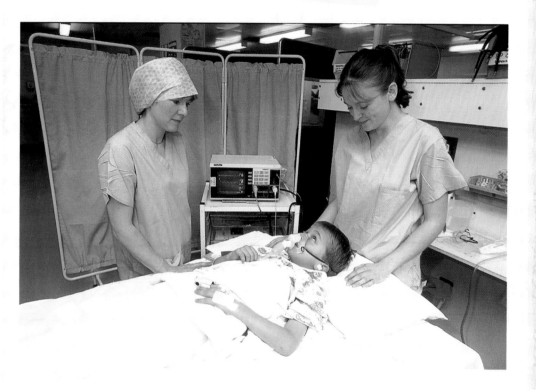

I wake up in a bright room.
The nurses smile and say hello.
I have cotton wool in my ears.
I am glad my operation is over.

We go back to the ward.

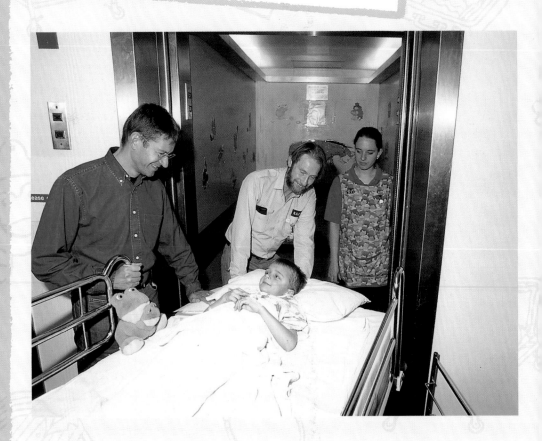

Dad and Hazel come and find me.
We go back to the ward. A porter
takes us in a lift.

Dad reads me a story.

I still feel a bit sleepy. Dad reads me a story and Hazel

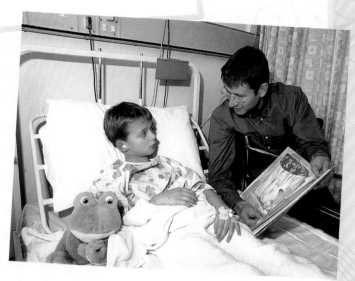

brings me a drink and some toast. Soon I feel better.

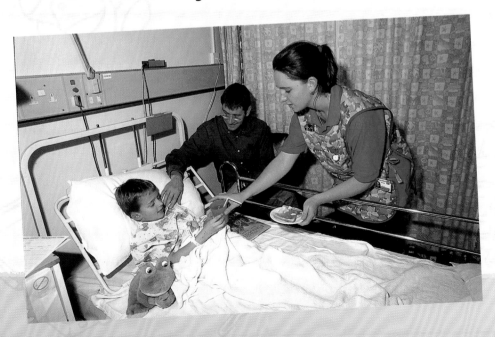

Mum is glad I am better.

Hazel says Dad and I can go to the playroom. Mum comes and finds me there. She is glad I am better.

I am going home.

I am going home now. I say goodbye to Hazel. My parents give her some flowers. I enjoyed my first visit to hospital.

Index

Notes to Parents and Teachers

Hospitalisation can be a stressful experience for both adults and children. Children will be worried about being away from home and anxious about suffering pain from operations and injections.

Much has been done in recent years to make hospitals more child-friendly. Children's wards are bright, cheerful places. Parents can stay with their children virtually all the time - including overnight, and pain relief has become more sophisticated and accessible.

Parents and teachers can do much to allay the fears of children before they go to hospital. Small children may believe that hospital is a punishment, so try to reassure them that nobody is cross with them. It is usually possible for a child to visit the hospital in advance to see where they will be staying and many hospitals have Play Specialists who are trained to prepare the child for a particular procedure or operation. Teachers may be able to hold a class discussion about hospital with contributions from children who have already experienced a stay in hospital. If in hospital for any length of time, children will appreciate cards and news from their class and being kept up to date with school work by their teacher.

- Don't prepare the child too far ahead - two to three days should be sufficient for a three to five-year-old.

- Never pretend the child is going somewhere else.

- Reassure the child that Mum/Dad can stay with them at all times.

- Take the child's favourite toy, blanket, mug, etc with you to hospital.

- Ensure the child understands what is going to happen. Most children's fear of hospital comes from not knowing or understanding what is going to happen, why they are there and whether it will hurt.

- Consulting children and allowing them to make small choices about their care will help them feel more relaxed and less frustrated.

For further information and support please contact:
Action for Sick Children, 300 Kingston Road, London, SW20 8LX
e-mail: ACTION_FOR_SICK_CHILDREN_EDU@MSN.COM
Web site: http://www.actionforsickchildren.org.uk